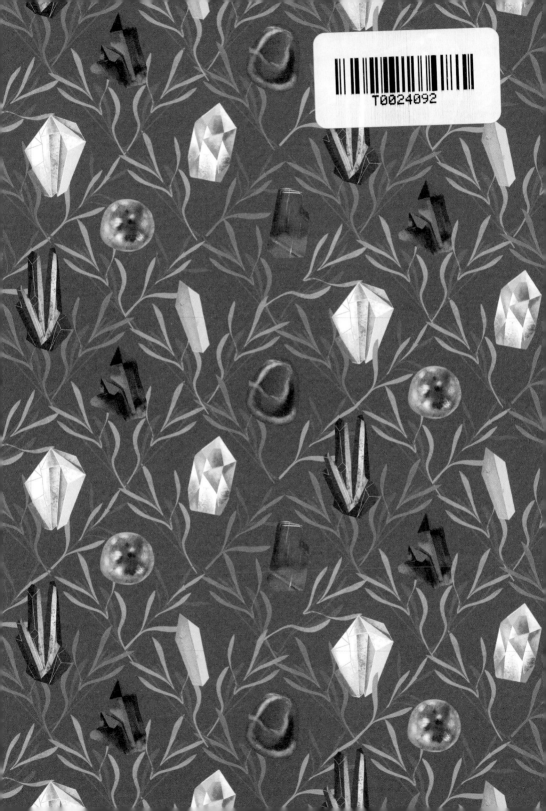

CRAFTING MAGIC

·····

A JUNIOR WITCH'S
GRIMOIRE

NIKKI VAN DE CAR
Illustrated by **UTA KROGMANN**

RP|KIDS
PHILADELPHIA

SAFETY FIRST!
Ask an adult before using matches or lighting candles or incense.
Never leave a candle unattended. Handle spell supplies and tools carefully
and don't make substitutions. If you are not sure,
ask for help with spell directions.

Running Press Kids
Hachette Book Group
1290 Avenue of the Americas, New York, NY 10104
www.runningpress.com/rpkids
@runningpresskids

Distributed in the United Kingdom by Little, Brown Book Group UK,
Carmelite House, 50 Victoria Embankment, London, EC4Y 0DZ

Printed in China

First Edition: March 2024

Published by Running Press Kids, an imprint of Hachette Book Group, Inc.
The Running Press Kids name and logo are trademarks of
Hachette Book Group, Inc.

The Hachette Speakers Bureau provides a wide range of authors for speaking
events. To find out more, go to www.hachettespeakersbureau.com
or email HachetteSpeakers@hbgusa.com.

Running Press books may be purchased in bulk for business,
educational, or promotional use. For more information, please contact your
local bookseller or the Hachette Book Group Special Markets Department
at Special.Markets@hbgusa.com.

The publisher is not responsible for websites (or their content)
that are not owned by the publisher.

Print book cover and interior design by Frances J. Soo Ping Chow.

ISBN: 978-0-7624-8452-2 (paperback)

APS

10 9 8 7 6 5 4 3 2 1

This
GRIMOIRE
BELONGS TO:

CONTENTS

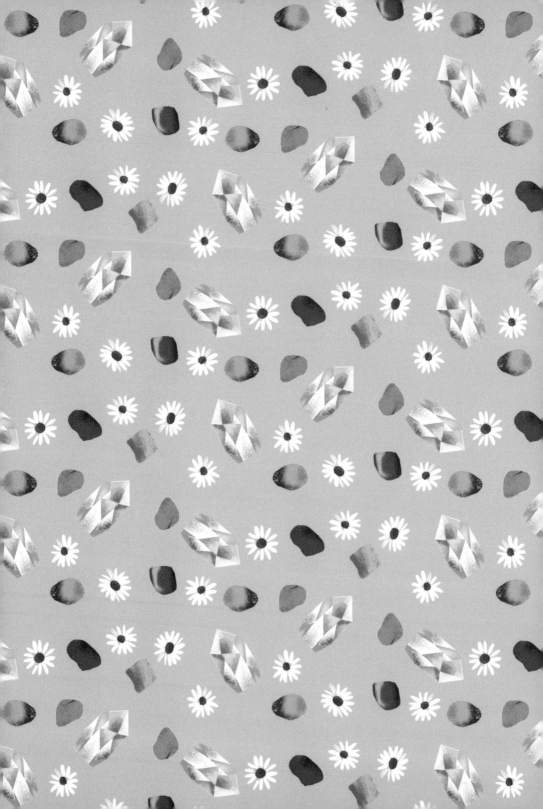

INTRODUCTION

Magic is based on something incredibly simple: intention. If you mean for something to be true, then it is. If you chant a spell, but you don't actually believe in it or really put your soul into it, then nothing will happen. But you can still yourself and say nothing at all while really *feeling* what you want to create, and that can be the most powerful magic of all. It all comes from you.

There is magic all around us, and it is created *by us* and *for us*. It is in the air we breathe and the ground we pass over, in the space between what we wish were true and what we *make* true. Accessing this magic requires imagination, creativity, a connection with the earth, and, most of all, a sense of curiosity and possibility within your heart.

This spellbook is here to support you as you grow your magical practice. It includes some sample spells, as well as prompts to inspire you to write your own. It includes basic herb magic, crystals, rituals, and meditations—but each of them can be adapted to suit your own needs. It's up to you to use your imagination and intuition to expand your magic, until you are creating your own spells and your own rituals as you grow into your powers.

This grimoire is organized into three sections: Friendship, Fulfillment, and Family, the three areas of our lives that have the most impact on us and that require the most of us. Within our spellwork, we focus on three areas: Creating, Healing, and Empowering. Creation magic means looking inside yourself for what you truly desire and then setting intentions toward making those desires into reality.

Healing magic is always necessary, because life isn't always easy—we get our feelings hurt, and even when we don't mean to, we hurt others as well. Spells of healing and forgiveness are an important part of any witch's magical practice.

Empowering magic is to help you live up to all of your potential, being all that you are capable of. Sometimes we think, *I can't do it* or *I'm not strong enough* . . . and spells for empowerment will support you in fighting against those thoughts and reclaiming your own personal energy.

Sometimes you may not have the ingredients you need for a particular spell on hand, and that's okay! You can make any substitutions you like; just keep track of them in this grimoire. The Table of Correspondences on pages XXI–XXIII will help you come up with any replacements you might need.

Sample Spell Record

• • • • • •

NAME OF SPELL
Give your spell a name you'll remember!

DATE/TIME/PLACE
For example: 2/14/XX, 3:30 p.m., bedroom

INTENTION OF SPELL
What is your spell for? Be clear about your intentions.

MATERIALS REQUIRED
Write down any tools, herbs, crystals, etc., that you used.

INCANTATION
If you spoke any words, either aloud or in your heart,
jot them down here.

Sample Ritual Record

• • ● • • •

NAME OF RITUAL

Write down the name of your ritual.

DATE/TIME/PLACE

For example: 2/14/XX, 3:30 p.m., bedroom

INTENTION OF RITUAL

Because rituals can be a little vaguer than spells, be sure to set very clear intentions each time you perform this ritual.

MATERIALS REQUIRED

Write down any tools, herbs, crystals, etc., that you used.

ACTION

Write down the process of your ritual, step-by-step, so you can remember it for next time.

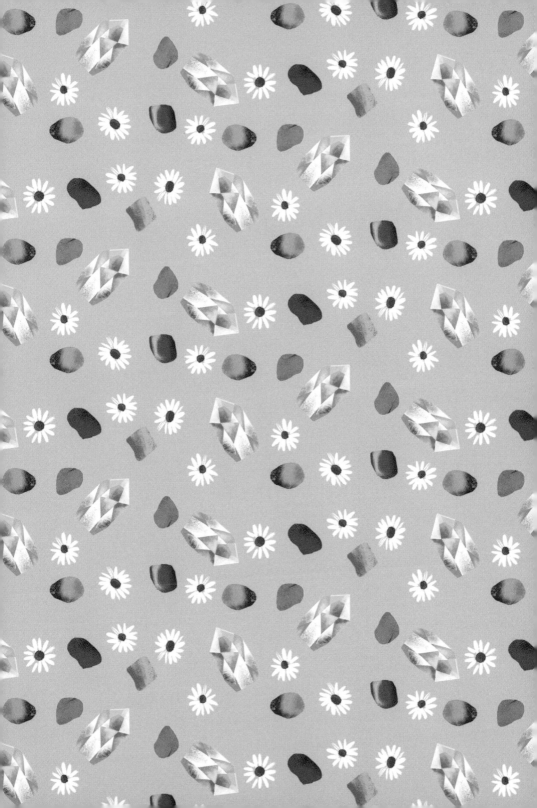

THINGS YOU'LL NEED

Altar

To create your altar—the physical representation of your overall magical practice—start by choosing a central symbol. It can be a photograph or some other image of someone you love, an ancestor, or even a goddess. You could use a bowl or chalice if you want to focus on inviting positive energies into your life or an incense burner if you want to disperse negative energies. You could use a large, powerful crystal to center your energy—anything that feels right. This kind of magic is very personal and very dependent on your own intuition. And remember, your decision is not final—this is just what your altar will look like today. You can change it around whenever you want.

You may also want to incorporate the elements, as the foundations of the natural world are also the building blocks of any magical practice. Here are some possibilities:

FIRE

Candle

Volcanic stones

Incense

AIR

Feather

Essential oil diffuser

Eggshells

WATER

Seashell

Mirror

Jar of rainwater

EARTH

Horn or bone

Sedimentary rock

Pottery

From here, get creative and have fun with it! Place things on your altar and remove them when they no longer feel right. You can add things you find, like buttons or lost keys, pieces of friendship bracelets, essential oils, bits of cloth, crystals, dried herbs—anything and everything you want.

When you're working on a big spell or focusing your energy toward something you really want, spend a little time with your altar, rearranging it and redecorating it. It'll help you align your desires with your power.

Crystals

CHUNK CRYSTAL. This includes geodes, pyrite, turquoise, or any kind of untouched crystal that looks basically the same way it did when it came out of the earth. These are often viewed as really useful knickknacks—you can keep them around your desk or in your room, providing your space with clarity, peace, protection, or whatever that particular crystal is best known for.

CUT CRYSTAL. Diamonds and other gems used in jewelry are cut to enhance their sparkle and capture light. They are very pretty, and often very powerful, as their impurities have been trimmed away.

TUMBLED. These are the stones you can often find in bins at a science or mystical shop. They're softer, often rounded, and are likely to be the crystals you use most in your daily magic practice.

WAND. This type is of crystal is shaped a bit like a literal wand, so that it's pointy at one end. You will find these useful in targeting the crystal's energies. In particular, a selenium or clear quartz wand is used to activate a crystal grid. A crystal grid is a geometric arrangement of complementary crystals—the shape helps them come into resonance with each other and amplifies their powers.

• • • • • •

Your stones will require some care and feeding! They work by taking on and releasing energy, but that means that you need to clear those energies and then recharge your crystals fairly often. Do this as soon as you purchase a stone, clearing any energies it may have picked up along its way to you, and then repeat that process once it's been used, so that it's ready for the next time you need it.

CLEARING. You can do this in a number of ways! You can wave a smoking herbal bundle over it or soak it in salt water overnight. You can hold it in a stream or in the rain, or you can leave it by a window to let it be washed by sunshine or moonlight.

CHARGING. For general charging, you can simply hold your crystal to your heart or your third eye (on your forehead, right between your eyebrows) and visualize its magic—its protection, its love, its healing. Feel that magic within yourself and within the crystal. Feel that interplay between the two of you. Then gently place the crystal wherever it is you keep it, knowing that it is ready for you whenever you need it.

Herbs

Like crystals, certain herbs have certain properties and can be used to amplify our own abilities. Often herbs are used in a gris-gris, or a small bag that can be used as a talisman. You can consume edible herbs as tea, which is, of course, a kind of potion.

You can also create an herbal bundle to use before conducting a spell or ritual. An herbal bundle is a small bound bunch of dried plants that you light on fire to activate their specific virtues. To create an herbal bundle, collect the fresh or dried herbs of your choice, and lay them together into a grouping about five inches long and maybe an inch or two thick. Wind cotton string or yarn tightly around your bundle, moving up and down the length of the stems, until you have a nice compacted stick. If you've used fresh plants, you'll need to hang your herbal bundle to dry for at least a week before using.

When it's ready, light the tip, but then blow it out so it's just smoldering—you don't need a licking flame. Wave your herbal bundle over a crystal grid or around the space where you'll be casting your spell, or let it rest on a dish and allow its smoke to move around you.

Essential Oils

Sometimes a spell will call for the same plant in either herb or essential oil form. The truth is that both are equally powerful, but they have different uses. Essential oils are a distilled version of the plant; they capture its aroma as well as its magical properties—literally its "essence." So it would take a handful of dried lavender to achieve the same power as a drop of lavender essential oil. Also, a number of essential oils are hard to find in fresh or dried form! When's the last time you saw myrrh or frankincense at the supermarket?

Look for therapeutic-grade oil, but don't stress about how highly rated it is—you don't need the most expensive ones. And no matter what, don't ever drink your essential oils! Even essential oils made from herbs we normally eat, like sage or thyme, can be toxic in this form because they are so very intense. Some of them, like lemon or lime, shouldn't be used directly on your skin, while others like chamomile or rose are gentle enough and can even be good for your skin, which is a nice bonus. More often, though, you'll use your essential oils to anoint candles or crystals.

TABLE OF CORRESPONDENCES

If you don't have all the ingredients you need for a particular spell, this table will help you substitute a different crystal, herb, or essential oil. If you don't have any of the herbs, you could just work in a crystal—remember, this is *your* spell, and you get to decide how it operates!

LIFE SKILL	HERBS	CRYSTALS	ESSENTIAL OILS
Balance	Alyssum, sunflower, lavender	Clear quartz, moonstone, pearl	Cedarwood, geranium, lavender
Boundaries	Hawthorn, yarrow, basil	Tigereye, pyrite, hematite	Basil, neroli, palo santo
Communication	Mint, parsley, yarrow	Aquamarine, blue calcite, blue apatite	Lavender, sage, neroli
Compassion	Marjoram, angelica, rose, hibiscus, violet	Rose quartz, malachite, jade, green aventurine	Rose, bergamot
Concentration	Rosemary, mint, sage, cinnamon	Amethyst, lapis lazuli, smoky quartz	Frankincense, myrrh, rosemary, lemon
Confidence	Fennel, motherwort, sunflower	Pyrite, yellow jasper, tigereye, citrine	Ginger, lemon

Courage	Black cohosh, garlic, yarrow, Saint-John's-wort	Amber, carnelian, garnet, red jasper	Myrrh, cinnamon, palo santo, sweet orange
Creativity	Tomato, vervain, ylang-ylang	Opal, garnet, carnelian	Jasmine, sandalwood
Divination	Holly, marigold, mugwort, wormwood	Opal, moonstone, lapis lazuli, amethyst	Lavender, rosemary, frankincense
Energy	Allspice, cinnamon, lime, lemon	Calcite, citrine, clear quartz, jade, opal, tigereye	Ginger, lemon, lime, sweet orange
Friendship	Crocus, evening primrose, cardamom	Rose quartz, malachite, green aventurine	Rose, bergamot, ginger
Harmony	Basil, marjoram, lemon balm	Carnelian, malachite, clear quartz	Rose, bergamot, lavender
Healing	Allspice, aloe, cinnamon, violet	Amethyst, clear quartz, turquoise, obsidian	Angelica, cloves, lavender
Intuition	Goldenrod, eyebright, yarrow	Amazonite, lapis lazuli, smoky quartz	Lavender, frankincense, myrrh
Luck	Allspice, clover, almond, cinquefoil	Agate, amazonite, amber, moonstone, peridot	Mint, cloves
Meditation	Acacia, anise, chamomile	Calcite, obsidian, amethyst, lapis lazuli	Frankincense, lavender, myrrh
Peace	Alyssum, basil, violet, chamomile, lemon balm	Moonstone, rose quartz, turquoise, hematite, azurite, aquamarine	Lavender, rose, chamomile

TABLE OF CORRESPONDENCES

Protection	Yarrow, basil, parsley	Hematite, smoky quartz, obsidian	Palo santo, pine, neroli
Rest	Lemon balm, vervain, yarrow, rue	Amethyst, clear quartz, malachite, moonstone	Lavender, chamomile
Strength	Garlic, mint, parsley, thyme	Fossil, garnet, hematite	Pine, tea tree oil, sweet orange
Wisdom	Apple, witch hazel, vervain	Amethyst, lapis lazuli, clear quartz	Sage, lavender, rosemary

FRIENDSHIP MAGIC

Our friends can often be the most important people in our lives. They laugh with us, cry with us, support us, and teach us.

Part of what makes them so special is that we have *chosen* them. It's such an incredible thing, when you think about it—out of all the people you know, you have found these three or four people (or ten or twelve, if you're the outgoing sort!) that really get you and you can really connect with. You have so much in common, whether it's similar tastes in books and TV shows or just a way of looking at the world.

You chose them, and they chose you.

There is power in that choice—but power always goes two ways. You can be incredibly close with your friends, but still have moments when, whether intentionally or not, they hurt your feelings or you hurt theirs.

Friendships require care, thoughtfulness, and intention—but if you put the necessary work in, you can have a relationship that is meaningful, supportive, and so much fun.

Creating Friendship Spell Bag

......

This spell can come in handy when you've moved to another town, another school, or if you just feel like there's a gap somewhere—maybe you have an interest your other friends don't share and it would be great to have someone to enjoy it with!

Start by taking a piece of paper and writing down the characteristics you're looking for in this new friendship. Do you want someone who is imaginative? Someone who is into music? Someone who likes karate? Is this person going to be kind, outgoing, studious, hilarious? Write it all down, then fold your piece of paper up nice and small.

Create a spell bag by cutting a two- or three-inch square of cloth. Choose your cloth carefully—do you want something soft or sparkly? What color feels right? Follow your intuition here, as you think about the kind of friend you want to invite into your life.

Place the piece of paper on the cloth. If you want, you can add some rose quartz or malachite and sprinkle the cloth with a bit of rose or ginger essential oil. Bring the edges together and tie it up with a ribbon. Make sure it's nice and tight.

For the next three nights, sleep with the bag beneath your pillow or next to your heart so that your unconscious mind can work its power.

You should know, though, that your new friend may show up in unexpected ways. You may find that you meet *exactly* the person you envisioned right after those three nights' sleep, or it may take a while longer. You might even find that an old friend, someone you've known forever, is suddenly different, more exciting—as if they suddenly are all the things you were looking for when you worked your spell.

Friendship Connection Ritual

• • • • • •

Consider forming a ritual for connection, something to seal your friendship. Pick a nice, sunny day, because you'll definitely want to be outside for this. Find a patch of grass, anywhere you can really get down low and touch the earth itself, with nothing between you. Sit in a circle with your friend(s)—it can be just two of you or as many as you like! You'll want to sit cross-legged, so that your knees are touching. For this ritual, think about the following:

- What you want to call forth in your friendship
- What crystals or herbs might support you
- What you might want to recite or chant

Friendship Code

······

Create a secret code or alphabet you can use to communicate with your friends—something no one else will be able to decipher! You can use runes, shifting letters so that A = D, B = E, C = F and so forth, or make up your own symbols!

Creating Friendship Spell

● ● ● ● ● ●

When you make a new friend or are reconnected with an old friend you haven't seen in a while, it can be a good idea to take a moment to honor that. Maybe you'll want to exchange crystals or offer a small blessing—and this can just be in your head! Sometimes, your magic is just for you.

Healing Friendship

●●•●●●

Sometimes, without meaning to, our friends can cross a line. They can be hurtful or demanding, and we can feel that we are giving more than we are receiving. This doesn't necessarily make them a bad friend—in fact, often they have absolutely no idea they are hurting us until we lash out at them. It can start with something really small, like borrowing a book. It's a book you love, one that you really want your friend to read and enjoy! And they loved it, too—until they lost it.

Okay, these things happen. But then they want to borrow a sweater and get paint on it. You tell them it's fine, not to worry. But if these types of things start happening over and over, you feel like they don't care about *you* if they're treating your stuff in this way.

Now let's think about it from their perspective. They probably assume you didn't like that sweater that much anyway, if you didn't mind that they got paint on it. They certainly haven't been keeping track of how many things of yours they've lost or ruined, or they haven't realized it bothered you—because you didn't tell them. If you yell, they get hurt and angry, too, because for them, this is coming out of nowhere and feels like an overreaction.

We've all been in these kinds of situations, on both sides. The way to avoid them is to react *sooner*, before you're upset.

Healing Friendship Meditation

•••••

This meditation practice will help you tune in to anger you may not even know you're feeling so that you can hear what it's trying to say and act on it before it starts shouting at you—and making you shout at other people.

On a day when a friend has bothered you, find a quiet space, somewhere without distractions. Sit comfortably and hold some tigereye or pyrite in your nondominant hand, palm closed around it. (Your nondominant hand is the one you *don't* write with. That's your left hand if you're right-handed or your right hand if you're left-handed.) Now, tune in to what you're feeling. It's okay; it can't harm anyone. Even though you told your friend you weren't bothered, ask yourself: *Am I bothered?*

Now ask yourself *what exactly* bothers you. In the example of the ruined stuff, it's not really the *stuff* that's the issue; it's the sense that if your friend cares so little for your things, how much do they really care about you? You may fight against exploring this feeling, because you do know how good a friend they are in so many other ways. But allowing yourself to feel this emotion doesn't change that; you can know that they're a good friend *and* have hurt feelings at the same time.

In this space of knowing your friend cares about you and knowing that they're not doing a great job of showing it in this instance, find your balance between the two. Get comfortable with it. Breathe slowly in and out, allowing yourself to find peace.

When you feel nice and relaxed, open your eyes. What you've done here is taken the emotion—the anger and hurt—out of the situation. Now you can calmly tell your friend, "Hey, I want you to take better care of my stuff" without being angry and without feeling hurt. That way, they can hear what you're saying without getting angry too. And it'll stay no big deal.

Spell to Release Anger

· · ● · · ·

When you want to stop feeling angry with your friend(s), take the time to write out everything you like about them—big things and little things. You'll find that you've filled an entire page before you know it. Decide what you want to do with this list—will you keep it under your pillow? Will you recite it as a spell?

Letting Go Spell

••••••

If you don't feel ready to have a conversation with your friend talking about what went wrong, try it here on these pages first. Write out an imaginary conversation, where you describe in detail what's bothering you. Then imagine their response. Really put yourself in their shoes. What do you think they would have to say? Use this imaginary conversation as a spell, a way to diffuse some of the hurt, and use your intuition to empathize. It will make the actual conversation so much easier. Use your magic to dispel some of the negative energy around your argument.

Healing Friendship Spell

•••••

Gather some amethyst, clear quartz, violets, and salt, or whatever other materials seem right for your spell on forgiveness and compassion. Use them to create a sacred circle and sit inside it.

Close your eyes, and let yourself really feel all the anger and all the hurt you've been holding on to. In order to process your feelings, you have to let them in. And then—let everything out. As you breathe in new air, visualize a fresh start, and as you exhale, visualize expelling all the pain and anger. Your hurt is held by the sacred circle, and it is fine to leave it there.

How do you want to close the spell? What can you use to add more peace, more acceptance, and more love?

Empowering Friendship Spell

• • ▪ ▪ • •

Did you know that friendship bracelets—those things we've all worn and given to each other—are rooted in some of the oldest magic there is? Knot magic is the act of tying literal knots into a cord or a piece of thread and using it to bind a spell. Sailors would use knot magic to bind winds and would untie the knots when they were becalmed or needed an extra boost.

Knot magic is not permanent, as it can be untied—but that's what makes it perfect for friendship magic. Remember, friendship is a *choice,* one that we make again and again. You and your friends have chosen each other, and these knots can be a symbol of that choice.

Start by picking the right materials. What best represents your friend? Are they into unicorns and sparkles and purple? Then perhaps some spangly yarn would be the way to go. Is your friend more of the adventurous type? Maybe some leather cord would be good. Give it some thought.

Magic often works best in threes, so start by writing down three or six or nine—or some other multiple of three—things you and your friend share. Then take your cord and tie a knot for the first connection you have together, speaking it aloud. You can then string on a bead or anything else that feels right. Then tie the next knot, for the next connection, again speaking it aloud. Repeat until all your knots are in place.

From there, if you want, you can turn your knot magic into a piece of jewelry! If it's small, make it a bracelet, or it can be worn as a necklace. Give it as a gift, as a symbol of your friendship, or get the group together so you make a bunch of them together, for each other!

Empowering Crystal Grid

• • • • • •

If you and your friends are working on a project, create a crystal grid together! Choose the crystals that best support the magic you are doing, and be creative, working together, sharing ideas, and taking turns placing the crystals until it feels representative of your combined magics.

List some of the crystals you used here:

Empowering Friendship Spell Bag

• • • • • •

If your friend needs some support, what can you do for them? Do you want to make them a spell bag? Cut a four-inch square of cloth in your friend's favorite color, and fill it with dried mint, rose quartz, or malachite. Finally, add something special. For example, if your friend is into science, add a drawing of oxytocin, the love molecule. You could create a tiny stuffed animal of their favorite creature. Give it some thought to choose what feels right, but make it small so that it fits in the spell bag. Cut a length of ribbon or twine, close the edges of the bag, and tie it tight.

Friendship Binding Spell

• • • • • •

What is something you really want to celebrate? What brings you and your friend(s) together? It can be a favorite musician or shared interest, a shared sense of humor, even a love of spooky stories! For this spell, you might want to ask everyone to contribute an object and a phrase that represents, for them, the connection you have. What kind of magic can you work to bind each other together?

Spell Record

• • ● • •

NAME OF SPELL

DATE/TIME/PLACE

INTENTION OF SPELL

MATERIALS REQUIRED

INCANTATION

Spell Record

• • • • • •

NAME OF SPELL

DATE/TIME/PLACE

INTENTION OF SPELL

MATERIALS REQUIRED

INCANTATION

Spell Record

• • ◉ • •

NAME OF SPELL

DATE/TIME/PLACE

INTENTION OF SPELL

MATERIALS REQUIRED

INCANTATION

Spell Record

· · • · ·

NAME OF SPELL

DATE/TIME/PLACE

INTENTION OF SPELL

MATERIALS REQUIRED

INCANTATION

Spell Record

· · • · ·

NAME OF SPELL

DATE/TIME/PLACE

INTENTION OF SPELL

MATERIALS REQUIRED

INCANTATION

Spell Record

• • • • • •

NAME OF SPELL

DATE/TIME/PLACE

INTENTION OF SPELL

MATERIALS REQUIRED

INCANTATION

Spell Record

• • • • •

NAME OF SPELL

DATE/TIME/PLACE

INTENTION OF SPELL

MATERIALS REQUIRED

INCANTATION

Spell Record

• • ● • •

NAME OF SPELL

DATE/TIME/PLACE

INTENTION OF SPELL

MATERIALS REQUIRED

INCANTATION

Spell Record

• • • • • •

NAME OF SPELL

DATE/TIME/PLACE

INTENTION OF SPELL

MATERIALS REQUIRED

INCANTATION

Spell Record

• • • • • •

NAME OF SPELL

DATE/TIME/PLACE

INTENTION OF SPELL

MATERIALS REQUIRED

INCANTATION

Ritual Record

• • ● • •

NAME OF RITUAL

DATE/TIME/PLACE

INTENTION OF RITUAL

MATERIALS REQUIRED

ACTION

Ritual Record

• • • • • •

NAME OF RITUAL

DATE/TIME/PLACE

INTENTION OF RITUAL

MATERIALS REQUIRED

ACTION

Ritual Record

•• • ••

NAME OF RITUAL

DATE/TIME/PLACE

INTENTION OF RITUAL

MATERIALS REQUIRED

ACTION

Ritual Record

•••••

NAME OF RITUAL

DATE/TIME/PLACE

INTENTION OF RITUAL

MATERIALS REQUIRED

ACTION

Ritual Record

· · ● · · ·

NAME OF RITUAL

DATE/TIME/PLACE

INTENTION OF RITUAL

MATERIALS REQUIRED

ACTION

Ritual Record

• • ● • •

NAME OF RITUAL

DATE/TIME/PLACE

INTENTION OF RITUAL

MATERIALS REQUIRED

ACTION

Ritual Record

NAME OF RITUAL

DATE/TIME/PLACE

INTENTION OF RITUAL

MATERIALS REQUIRED

ACTION

Ritual Record

•• •• • •

NAME OF RITUAL

DATE/TIME/PLACE

INTENTION OF RITUAL

MATERIALS REQUIRED

ACTION

Ritual Record

•• • • ••

NAME OF RITUAL

DATE/TIME/PLACE

INTENTION OF RITUAL

MATERIALS REQUIRED

ACTION

Ritual Record

• • ● • •

NAME OF RITUAL

DATE/TIME/PLACE

INTENTION OF RITUAL

MATERIALS REQUIRED

ACTION

NOTES

NOTES

NOTES

FULFILLMENT MAGIC

I t's possible you're not familiar with this word, but it's an important one to know.

FUL-FILL-MENT. *1. Satisfaction or happiness as a result of achieving something one desires. 2. Satisfaction or happiness as a result of fully developing one's abilities or character.*

Let's look at both definitions. With the first one, we may often think about work/school—about getting good grades or struggling through homework. Being successful in school *is* satisfying, and it can lead to a happy, productive adult life. Working hard is important.

And yet, that's not all there is to it. The second definition talks about working on ourselves, for ourselves—not for any specific life goal. Exploring concepts that spark our interest, learning new skills, and developing our talents are also hard work, and this also leads to happiness and satisfaction with your life—and perhaps more importantly, with yourself. That sometimes requires *divination*.

The word *divination* has two meanings: *1. To look into the future and literally see what's going to happen. 2. To use your intuition to gain insight into what will happen in the future.*

The first one is pretty unlikely, really. There are just too many possibilities in life—every choice you make can lead to hundreds of *new* choices that didn't exist before. That's really exciting, but it does make predicting the future a pretty inexact science. Divination spellwork won't give you a winning lottery number or tell you the name of your college roommate.

This section of your grimoire is a space to navigate and develop both those definitions of fulfillment, providing you with the inner strength to manage the inevitable ups and downs in life, the courage you need to try something new, as well as the creativity and insight you need to figure out what truly makes you happy.

Creating Fulfillment Spell

......

This divination spell won't show you the answers to your next math quiz or who will come to visit your house next week. Instead, it will help you look inside yourself, to divine what is right and true for *you*. What do you want to be when you grow up? What will make you happiest today? These are the kinds of questions you should ask when performing this spell.

Start by anointing a candle with lavender or frankincense essential oil—just don't get the wick wet! Place your candle on a small plate, and surround the base with opal, moonstone, or lapis lazuli crystals. If it's available, sprinkle some mugwort or wormwood around your candle, too. Light the candle, and sit so that you are bathed in its light.

Look at the candle and allow your thoughts to drift. Ask yourself, *What do I want?* Allow your imagination to drift, thinking about what your life *might* be like and what you might want. Keep going until the candle reaches the point where it starts to drip.

What were you thinking of at that moment? Write it down, and then wait and see! Perhaps that was your future at that moment, on that day, but it will shift because of a choice you are going to make tomorrow. Or maybe you are spot-on!

Fulfillment Intention Spell

•••••

Write down your deepest desire, whether it's to get into a certain school, go on a trip, perfect a new skill—whatever it may be. Fold the paper in half twice. Then take it outside and find a patch of clover. Carefully, lift the clover aside with its roots intact and place your paper beneath it. Pat the clover back in place and water it.

Over the next three days, visit your patch of clover. Stroke it, sing to it, and imagine your wish being granted. Put all that imagining into the clover, so that it is receiving your intention from above and from below.

Manifesting Fulfillment Spell

• • • • • •

Ask yourself, *What do I want? What makes me happy? What do I have to offer the world? What is the right choice?* These questions are frequently at the heart of all our struggles, and in truth, we can never really give a final answer for them. We change and evolve, and what is right *right now* may be wrong tomorrow. But it is in the asking that we get to know ourselves, even as we change. What are your answers today?

Crystals Fulfillment Ritual

• • • • •

Choose a crystal that connects you to your third eye chakra, the source of your intuition, like lapis lazuli, azurite, fluorite, fuchsite, lepidolite, sapphire, labradorite, or apophyllite. Lay down and place the crystal just above and between your eyebrows. Close your eyes and sit quietly until the crystal reaches your body temperature. As you wait, pay attention to what you see and what you feel. Let your third eye guide you, and when you can "see" your desires clearly, remove the crystal and set it aside. Write down what your intuition told you, and then keep the crystal nearby for a week or two—don't clear it yet, just let it be, retaining your energy and guidance.

Healing Fulfillment Meditation

• • • • • •

Fulfillment will never be achieved without some failure along the way. If it were easy, it wouldn't be all that fulfilling, would it? Failure is an integral part of the process of reaching satisfaction and happiness.

That doesn't mean it's a pleasant experience. Whenever we fail at something—and particularly when it's something we really want to be good at—it *hurts*. We feel all kinds of emotions and may decide that this failure along our journey means that we're not good at this (whatever *this* is), that we're never going to be good at this, and, sometimes, that's there's something wrong with *us* because we weren't successful this time.

It can help to take a step back and reassess things. Imagine that the person in this situation isn't *you*, but your best friend. You *know* this is just a minor setback. You *know* they've got this, and that if they were to give up now, you'd remind them to keep going.

Healing Fulfillment Spell

• • • • •

Gather some clear quartz, some lemon or lime essential oil, and a candle. Anoint the candle with your essential oil and light it. Hold your crystal in your palm.

Now, think about your failure. Ask yourself what you could have done differently. The question is not about blaming or about listing all the ways you screwed up; instead, it's literal information-gathering. You can't fix what went wrong unless you *know* what went wrong.

Offer yourself the comfort you would give your best friend. You know what you would say, and you know what you need to hear. You can be just as kind to yourself as you would be to them.

As you hold your crystal, imagine next time—because you know there will be a next time! Imagine how *awesome* you'll do then, and let your crystal absorb that image. Remember to consider the possibility that it won't be perfect then, either! New problems might come up, ones that you're not able to anticipate right now. Remind yourself in advance that if that happens, it's okay. It's just another step forward.

When you've filled your clear quartz with everything you need, blow out the candle. Let this failure go. It's done. Tuck the clear quartz somewhere for safekeeping so that it will be there to support you on your next try.

Spell to Harness the Moon

• • • • • •

The moon is a celestial body of mystery, of femininity and creativity. On the night of a full moon, harness her powers. Sit with your journal and a cup of tea. Allow the moonlight to shine on the page, and simply write down any thoughts that come to you. Be free and easy—you can skip punctuation and even grammar, as you simply let your mind flow. What do you want? What do you look forward to in life?

Lunar Cycle Inspiration

•• • • • •

For one full lunar cycle, write down a single word or phrase on this page every day. Don't put too much thought into it—just write down whatever comes to mind. At the end of the cycle, circle any common themes. What have you learned about yourself? What inspires you?

Healing Fulfillment Ritual

• • • • • •

When you've had a hard day, start by treating yourself. Give yourself a little gift to make it better. Watch your favorite movie. Read a book. Get some fresh air. Blow off a little steam. Go shopping. Don't mull over what went wrong, don't stew over it, and don't even think about how you'll do better next time—that's for later. Do something that feels *really good*.

We are often much more generous with others than we are with ourselves. This ritual will help you apply the same loving support, comfort, and encouragement to yourself that is so easy to give to others.

Empowering Fulfillment Potion

······

We all get distracted sometimes. It's impossible not to. We can blame the internet, phones, television, texting, but people have faced distractions since well before that, just by different things—birds and books, maybe? It's an eternal struggle.

The quickest and easiest method for improving concentration is to brew yourself a cup of tea.

Making tea may not sound like your idea of a potion, but think of it this way: tea is a potion; in fact, it's the most commonly brewed potion there is. It's a mixture of magical ingredients added to water that you then drink. There is so much magic to be found and cultivated in the making and drinking of tea.

For a full pot of tea, you'll want a combined tablespoon's worth of the following dried herbs. For just a cup, you'll only need a teaspoon. Blend together a mixture of:

- Rosemary, for memory
- Mint, for finding flow
- Sage, for wisdom
- Cinnamon stick, to enhance brain activity

Put it in a tea strainer, then let your tea steep for around 10 minutes. (If you're brewing just a mug, cover it so it doesn't get cold.) While it's steeping, surround it with amethyst, lapis lazuli, and smoky quartz, and when it's done, stir in honey and a squeeze of lemon.

Fulfillment Alignment Spell

••••••

Choose a crystal that connects you to your throat chakra, the source of your true voice, like aquamarine, turquoise, sodalite, or blue lace agate. Place it in the hollow at the base of your throat, gently holding it in place. Hum a little so that you can feel the vibration moving through. And now, *speak out*. What have you kept silent? What kind of spell do you need to cast to help you speak your truth?

Finding Fulfillment Ritual

••••••

Write a letter to your former self. Comfort yourself for mistakes you've made and remember to compliment yourself for the things you are proud of. Or write a letter to your future self. Put everything you wish for them into this letter, writing out your intentions for the person you will become. And now, what will you do with this letter? Should you bury it in the earth, and let Mama Earth support its growth? Should you let the wind take it? Should you burn it? Should you dissolve it in water?

Empowering Fulfillment Mist

• • • • • •

This potion isn't one that you drink. Instead, it's to spritz on your face (being careful not to get it in your eyes!), your hands, the back of your neck—anywhere that you feel you are carrying worry, frustration, or any other kind of negative energy. It will bring you a fresh burst of positivity.

In a small glass spray bottle, combine:

• 2 tablespoons witch hazel

• 10 drops lemon essential oil

• 10 drops sweet orange essential oil

• 10 drops peppermint essential oil

Fill any remaining space in the bottle with water, shake well, and give yourself an energetic and emotional boost whenever you need it.

Spell Record

• • • • • •

NAME OF SPELL

DATE/TIME/PLACE

INTENTION OF SPELL

MATERIALS REQUIRED

INCANTATION

Spell Record

• • • • • •

NAME OF SPELL

DATE/TIME/PLACE

INTENTION OF SPELL

MATERIALS REQUIRED

INCANTATION

Spell Record

• • ● • •

NAME OF SPELL

DATE/TIME/PLACE

INTENTION OF SPELL

MATERIALS REQUIRED

INCANTATION

Spell Record

· · • · ·

NAME OF SPELL

DATE/TIME/PLACE

INTENTION OF SPELL

MATERIALS REQUIRED

INCANTATION

Spell Record

•• • ••

NAME OF SPELL

DATE/TIME/PLACE

INTENTION OF SPELL

MATERIALS REQUIRED

INCANTATION

Spell Record

NAME OF SPELL

DATE/TIME/PLACE

INTENTION OF SPELL

MATERIALS REQUIRED

INCANTATION

Spell Record

......

NAME OF SPELL

DATE/TIME/PLACE

INTENTION OF SPELL

MATERIALS REQUIRED

INCANTATION

Spell Record

• • ● • •

NAME OF SPELL

DATE/TIME/PLACE

INTENTION OF SPELL

MATERIALS REQUIRED

INCANTATION

Spell Record

•• • •••

NAME OF SPELL

DATE/TIME/PLACE

INTENTION OF SPELL

MATERIALS REQUIRED

INCANTATION

Spell Record

• • ● • •

NAME OF SPELL

DATE/TIME/PLACE

INTENTION OF SPELL

MATERIALS REQUIRED

INCANTATION

Ritual Record

· · ● · ·

NAME OF RITUAL

DATE/TIME/PLACE

INTENTION OF RITUAL

MATERIALS REQUIRED

ACTION

Ritual Record

• • • • •

NAME OF RITUAL

DATE/TIME/PLACE

INTENTION OF RITUAL

MATERIALS REQUIRED

ACTION

Ritual Record

·· ● ··

NAME OF RITUAL

DATE/TIME/PLACE

INTENTION OF RITUAL

MATERIALS REQUIRED

ACTION

Ritual Record

· · • · ·

NAME OF RITUAL

DATE/TIME/PLACE

INTENTION OF RITUAL

MATERIALS REQUIRED

ACTION

Ritual Record

• • • • • •

NAME OF RITUAL

DATE/TIME/PLACE

INTENTION OF RITUAL

MATERIALS REQUIRED

ACTION

Ritual Record

•• • ••

NAME OF RITUAL

DATE/TIME/PLACE

INTENTION OF RITUAL

MATERIALS REQUIRED

ACTION

Ritual Record

• • • • • •

NAME OF RITUAL

DATE/TIME/PLACE

INTENTION OF RITUAL

MATERIALS REQUIRED

ACTION

Ritual Record

· · • · ·

NAME OF RITUAL

DATE/TIME/PLACE

INTENTION OF RITUAL

MATERIALS REQUIRED

ACTION

Ritual Record

• • • • • •

NAME OF RITUAL

DATE/TIME/PLACE

INTENTION OF RITUAL

MATERIALS REQUIRED

ACTION

Ritual Record

•••••

NAME OF RITUAL

DATE/TIME/PLACE

INTENTION OF RITUAL

MATERIALS REQUIRED

ACTION

NOTES

NOTES

NOTES

FAMILY
MAGIC

In so many ways, our families are the most important people in our lives. We see them every day, we live with them, eat with them, and no matter what, they will always be there, forever. Unlike with our friends, we don't get to *choose* them—this is the family we have, and for better or worse, we're stuck with them.

They can drive us crazy. Nobody can irritate you more or find ways to hit where you're most sensitive than your parents or siblings. And at the same time, no one can make you feel more loved or like you're seen for who you truly are than your family. They know us better than anyone else because they have seen every part of us. They *are* a part of us.

This kind of connection is so powerful, and yet so challenging, because it goes both ways. We can hurt or support the members of our family in all the same ways they can hurt or support us. In fact, these relationships are the ones most under our control. That golden rule about treating others as you wish to be treated? It works most of the time but is never more effective than when dealing with your family. Do you wish that your mom would assume the best of you? If you assume the best of her, you'll likely find that she responds in kind. Do you wish that your older brother would include you more? Share with him some of the interesting things you're doing, and as he realizes he actually enjoys your company, he'll spend less time ignoring you.

It doesn't *always* work and it certainly isn't easy—but families are worth the effort. This section will provide you with some spells, tools, and practices that will help you enjoy the good times, while also navigating the more stressful ones.

Family Connection Spell

•• •••

Sometimes we can feel really distant from those we love, even when they're right there. We can go about our days together, and not really *see* each other, as we cycle through the routines of morning rush-school-homework-dinner-bed. We can feel lonely even when we're surrounded by people who love us.

When this happens, try casting a gentle binding spell to help you sense that closeness again. Collect a few strands of your own hair and combine them with some hairs of the person—or persons!—you want to feel closer to. Hold them in your hands, and then tie them together in a knot.

Take the knot of hair outside, and bury it in the earth, where it can regenerate, change, and help create new life. As you do so, remember that you are bound by love, by living together day after day, and that nothing can ever break that connection.

And then, having been empowered by this spell, start being the change you want to see. Instead of watching television, go hang out with your sister. Help with dinner. Suggest a family game night. You have more impact than you realize and can make your family dynamic into exactly what you want it to be.

Family Constellation Chart

• • • • • •

Write a kind of family constellation. Start with your parents, and add in any siblings, partners, children—whatever feels like family to you. What roles do each of them play in your life? What roles do you serve in theirs? And then, once you know what is true for your family, consider what you might want to change. How can you support these shifts in yourself? What does your intuition tell you?

Memory Keeping Ritual

•••••

What is your earliest memory? It's likely to be fuzzy, and perhaps even a created memory from stories you've been told. But allow yourself some time to explore it. Why is this the first thing you remember? What's important about it? What does that tell you about your family? Use the gift of that memory to set an intention for how you want to grow and change.

Family Binding Spell

· · ● · ·

Sometimes family can include "found family." Who are the people in your life that feel closest to you, that know you best? They can be family, too. If you want, you can cast a spell together, sealing the relationship—spitting into your hands and shaking is a binding spell, after all! Or you can simply write their name or names here, acknowledging what they mean to you.

Family Sweetening Spell

• • • • • •

Sweetening spells have their roots in the voodoo traditions of New Orleans, and they're some of the most positive magic there is. They are used to "sweeten" a situation or relationship. If you've been fighting a lot with a sibling or grown-up, or just generally feel like you're butting heads all the time, this spell can help take out any bitterness you may be feeling and allow you to rediscover your love for each other.

Take a piece of paper and write the name of the person you're struggling with three times. Then rotate the paper 90 degrees and write your own name three times, so that they cross over the other person's. It will look like the letters are weaving together. Draw a circle around your interlocking names. Following the line of the circle, write what you want in the relationship. You could write:

- Laughter
- Joy
- Love

- Fun
- Support
- Trust

Or any combination of the above works, too. But—and this is both important and kind of fun—you must write in a continuous line. Write in cursive, or without lifting your pen or pencil from the paper. Don't worry about dotting your I's and crossing your t's. So *laughter* over and over might look like: laughterlaughterlaughter laughter.

Continue until the circle is complete.

When you're finished, fold the paper in half again and again until it's nice and small. Take a small jar of honey, dip in a tea-spoon, and make room for your piece of paper. Remember, part of sweetening a relationship will include sweetening yourself, so take a taste. Then insert your folded paper into the jar and seal it up tight.

Ancestral Connection Spell

• • ■ • • •

Imagine an ancestor from many generations back—someone you've never met. What are they like? How does their nature support and inform yours? What could you learn from each other? Perhaps you might use a candle or your third eye to form a connection with this ancestor and allow your psychic abilities to help you access their wisdom.

Healing Family Meditation

• • • • •

This active, waking meditation can be done even in the middle of an argument, sitting on the sidelines while someone else is fighting, or just in the general anxiety of living with people we love. All you need to do is to put your attention on five things that are outside of the stressful moment. Doing this will clear out the cobwebs of your anxieties and frustrations, allowing you to see clearly—and communicate clearly, too.

Healing Family Ritual

• • • • • •

Sometimes, when you're having a hard time, it can seem like no one is on your side—and certainly not your family. When you start to feel a little "me against the world," perform this ritual with your family to remind yourself that you're not alone. There's a whole family—a whole world—full of positive energy working for you and for those who love you. Put together a playlist of your family's favorite songs—get three from each member—and spend an evening listening to each other's music—singing along if you know the words, dancing if you feel like it—recognizing the ways in which you each contribute, the ways in which you're different, and how you complement each other.

Empowering Family Spell

•• • ••

When you feel like you and your family are in a bit of a rut, that you're having a hard time communicating with each other, that everyone's stressed all the time and just kind of going through the motions of school-work-eat-sleep without really enjoying each other, try this spell.

If it's something your family wants to do with you, that's great, but they don't need to. As always, you have everything you need, all by yourself. For this spell, start by clearing all the negative energy that is present. Use a sage herbal bundle to clear the air, or even just meditate for a moment, concentrating on dissipating all of those messy, stressful feelings.

Use a selenium wand to draw a sacred circle around you and anyone else that might be participating in the spell. If you're alone, sit cross-legged, with your palms open on your knees, but if you have someone with you, sit across from each other or in a circle and hold hands.

Take three deep, cleansing breaths together. Then list three things you love about each of the members of your family—and then list three things you know they love about you, too. If you're in a group, have everyone take turns doing this. If you're alone, place your hands on your heart and say, "I love you, I love you, I love you." If you're together with your family, squeeze each other's hands tight, and say it in a chorus, all together.

Finally—hug it out! If some or all of your family is there with you, get in on a big group hug. If you've done the spell alone, make time throughout the rest of the day to hug each member of your family, if you can. You don't have to give them a reason, just put all your love into your arms and your heart. For anyone who isn't around, hug yourself with your arms tight, and send them your hug energetically. They'll feel it, even if they don't know where it's coming from.

Family Guardian Spell

• • ▪ • •

While we are the best source of our own power and magic, it can be useful to channel that energy into an object, so that it can protect and empower your home and family even when your attention is elsewhere. This object will act as a guardian for your home, watching over you and those you love, as you imbue it with the power of that love.

Familiar Binding Ritual

• • • • • •

A witch's familiar doesn't necessarily have to be a black cat. It can be any creature at all—a deer, a dog, a dragonfly, anything. What makes a creature your familiar is your relationship—they support you and the magic you work in the world. Who might your familiar be? What ritual can you perform to bind and seal your relationship with your familiar?

Empowering Family Candle Magic

• • ■ • •

This spell is intended to help you and your family feel completely *yourselves*—who you are, without judgment, standing fully in your power. Select a red candle (red is for courage). Crush a clove of garlic and rub its oil on the outside of the candle. Place agate, bloodstone, sardonyx, or tigereye near the candle, and put all this on the floor or a table where all the members of your family can gaze into its flames. Watch it flicker, and then, taking turns, carefully hold your hands above the flame so that its heat forms a sharp point pressing into your palm—but don't burn yourselves! Once you've all felt the heat of the flame, hold hands, sealing that heat between you.

Spell Record

• • ● • •

NAME OF SPELL

DATE/TIME/PLACE

INTENTION OF SPELL

MATERIALS REQUIRED

INCANTATION

Spell Record

• • ● • •

NAME OF SPELL

DATE/TIME/PLACE

INTENTION OF SPELL

MATERIALS REQUIRED

INCANTATION

Spell Record

• • ● • •

NAME OF SPELL

DATE/TIME/PLACE

INTENTION OF SPELL

MATERIALS REQUIRED

INCANTATION

Spell Record

• • ◉ • •

NAME OF SPELL

DATE/TIME/PLACE

INTENTION OF SPELL

MATERIALS REQUIRED

INCANTATION

Spell Record

• • ● • •

NAME OF SPELL

DATE/TIME/PLACE

INTENTION OF SPELL

MATERIALS REQUIRED

INCANTATION

Spell Record

• • ● • •

NAME OF SPELL

DATE/TIME/PLACE

INTENTION OF SPELL

MATERIALS REQUIRED

INCANTATION

Spell Record

• • • • • •

NAME OF SPELL

DATE/TIME/PLACE

INTENTION OF SPELL

MATERIALS REQUIRED

INCANTATION

Spell Record

· · ● · ·

NAME OF SPELL

DATE/TIME/PLACE

INTENTION OF SPELL

MATERIALS REQUIRED

INCANTATION

Spell Record

• • • • • •

NAME OF SPELL

DATE/TIME/PLACE

INTENTION OF SPELL

MATERIALS REQUIRED

INCANTATION

Spell Record

• • ● • •

NAME OF SPELL

DATE/TIME/PLACE

INTENTION OF SPELL

MATERIALS REQUIRED

INCANTATION

Ritual Record

• • • • • •

NAME OF RITUAL

DATE/TIME/PLACE

INTENTION OF RITUAL

MATERIALS REQUIRED

ACTION

Ritual Record

• • ● • •

NAME OF RITUAL

DATE/TIME/PLACE

INTENTION OF RITUAL

MATERIALS REQUIRED

ACTION

Ritual Record

• • ● • •

NAME OF RITUAL

DATE/TIME/PLACE

INTENTION OF RITUAL

MATERIALS REQUIRED

ACTION

Ritual Record

· · • · ·

NAME OF RITUAL

DATE/TIME/PLACE

INTENTION OF RITUAL

MATERIALS REQUIRED

ACTION

Ritual Record

• • ● • •

NAME OF RITUAL

DATE/TIME/PLACE

INTENTION OF RITUAL

MATERIALS REQUIRED

ACTION

Ritual Record

• • ● • •

NAME OF RITUAL

DATE/TIME/PLACE

INTENTION OF RITUAL

MATERIALS REQUIRED

ACTION

Ritual Record

· · ● · ·

NAME OF RITUAL

- -

DATE/TIME/PLACE

- -

INTENTION OF RITUAL

- -

- -

MATERIALS REQUIRED

- -

- -

- -

ACTION

- -

- -

- -

- -

- -

Ritual Record

• • ● • • •

NAME OF RITUAL

DATE/TIME/PLACE

INTENTION OF RITUAL

MATERIALS REQUIRED

ACTION

Ritual Record

• • • • • •

NAME OF RITUAL

DATE/TIME/PLACE

INTENTION OF RITUAL

MATERIALS REQUIRED

ACTION

Ritual Record

•• • ••

NAME OF RITUAL

DATE/TIME/PLACE

INTENTION OF RITUAL

MATERIALS REQUIRED

ACTION

NOTES

NOTES

NOTES